YOUR KNOWLEDGE HAS VALUE

- We will publish your bachelor's and master's thesis, essays and papers

- Your own eBook and book - sold worldwide in all relevant shops

- Earn money with each sale

Upload your text at www.GRIN.com and publish for free

Mohammad AbuHmaid

The Attitudes of Teachers and Students about Using their Mother Tongue in learning English

In a Private School in Amman

GRIN Publishing

Bibliographic information published by the German National Library:

The German National Library lists this publication in the National Bibliography; detailed bibliographic data are available on the Internet at http://dnb.dnb.de .

Imprint:

Copyright © 2014 GRIN Verlag GmbH
Print and binding: Books on Demand GmbH, Norderstedt Germany
ISBN: 978-3-656-84768-7

This book at GRIN:

http://www.grin.com/en/e-book/284461/the-attitudes-of-teachers-and-students-about-using-their-mother-tongue

The Attitudes of Teachers and Students about Using L1 in the EFL Classrooms in a private School in Amman: Case Study

Muhammed AbuHmaid
The Schools of the Islamic Educational College, Amman-Jordan

Abstract

The aim of this study is to investigate the attitudes of the students' as well as the teachers' use of their mother tongue (henceforth L1) in learning English as a foreign language (henceforth EFL) classrooms amongst the students of The Schools of the Islamic Educational College. The use of the students' mother tongue in learning English as a foreign language has been controversial for a long time. There have been various opinions about the utilizing of L1 in EFL classrooms. Recently, it has been noticed that some teachers tend to use so much of their mother tongue (Arabic) in EFL classrooms which has been reflected to the students' tendency towards accepting this trend within an EFL classrooms. An attempt has been made to review the students' as well as the teachers' perspectives regarding this issue. A questionnaire has been distributed amongst the students to highlight the different opinions and reactions about the use of Arabic in their EFL lessons. In addition, teachers of the seventh and tenth grades and some students have been interviewed for the same purpose. The results showed that there are positive students' attitudes towards using Arabic in EFL classes. The students in the study preferred the use of Arabic for various situations and reasons. The target teachers show rigidity about the use of Arabic although they admit that a rare use of Arabic might exist in their classes under certain circumstances. Recommendations as well as some future solutions are discussed.

Introduction

I) Previous Studies

The use of students' first language in learning English as a foreign language has been a critical issue and a subject of question for a long time. Different linguists and scholars who have came up with new methods and approaches have shown their beliefs about advocating this trend or objecting it without having a thorough study investigating the learners' as well as the teachers' point of views. The main objections against using the students' mother tongue have been that it does not motivate and encourage learners to use the L2 and that too much use of the L1 deprives the learners of input in the L2 (Krashen 1982, Hawks 2001) which represents my style in teaching . However, others see that the use of L1 in classrooms may reduce anxiety and create more relaxing learning environment (i.e Auerbach, 1993). On a wider scale, Atkinson (1987) believes that the use of the mother tongue can facilitate checking understanding and giving instructions. Here, I say that if simple language is used during lessons would be better. In addition, as some think, explaining the meaning of abstract words and introducing the main differences in grammar and pronunciation between L1 and L2 would be easier (Buckmaster 2000). The main idea here is to save time and effort on the expenses of using the target language.

There have been a lot of studies and research papers concerning this issue without coming to a conclusion. In his article "The Mother Tongue in the classroom: a neglected resource?" (1987), David Atkinson makes the point that the potential of the students' mother tongue use in the classroom requires more and more exploration. He also claims that the gap in methodological literature is somehow responsible for teachers' hesitation and uneasiness about using the students' mother tongue or not in the classroom. Atkinson (1993) states that it is impossible to decide on the right balance for using L1 in EFL classes, but he adds that L1 can be a precious resource if it is used at appropriate times and ways. Ford (2009) also concluded that there seemed a view that the most dominant approach in EFL classes was English only as the main principle communicative methodologies. He found no proof or evidence of qualitative research concerning teachers' tendencies on this issue at Japanese Universities where they all reject the idea of using Japanese during English classes. Nation (2003) showed that the first language has a small but an important role in communicating meaning and content and here I would say if it is wisely and not habitually. It is noticed that only few studies concerning the use of Arabic in EFL classroom have been conducted in the Arab world. In her case study "The Attitudes Of Teachers And Students Towards Using of Arabic In EFL Classrooms In Saudi Public Schools", Al-Nofaie (2010) concluded that the results of her study revealed a positive attitude about the use of Arabic in the classroom by both students and teachers although teachers' attitudes sometimes contradict with those for the students. Here, I have to explain that both teachers and students in Saudi Arabia especially at public schools use Arabic more than English in EFL classes as I was a teacher at different schools there from 1996 to 2005. Alshammari's (2011) research results also indicates that a balanced use of Arabic by both teachers and learners can be beneficial in the language learning process and might increase the students' level of comprehension. Not much attention has been paid to the using L1 in the Jordanian EFL classroom. To explore this issue in Jordan, a study was conducted to tackle the views of the IECS teachers and students (ninth and tenth Grades) towards the use of Arabic in EFL classrooms.

II) Research Instruments and Procedures for Data Collection

In order to collect data from students and teachers, two methods have been applied to for this purpose: a questionnaire and interviews with teachers and students. The attitudes of the students have been investigated through questionnaire (Appendix A) consisting of fifteen questions measures their attitudes about using Arabic in EFL classes. The SPSS software have been used to give descriptive analysis of the questionnaire. The interviews with both teachers and students were analyzed qualitatively (Appendix B). A detailed description of the design and application of research instruments will be examined in the following sections.

a. Questionnaires:

The questions in the questionnaire (taken and modified from Al Nofaie, 2010) have been designed to measure the attitudes of the students about using L1 in EFL classrooms. The closed questions in the questionnaire and a frequency scale of five points (from always to never) have been used to have the opportunity to compare the responses of the students. The questionnaires have been distributed to 160 students.

b. Interviews:

To get more explanations about their attitudes, interviews with both teachers and students have been conducted to show their tendencies. The responses have been written down during the interviews. The questions of the interview have been open to explore more information which might not be shown from the results of the questionnaires. High as well as low achiever students have been chosen to explore different attitudes from students from different levels. Teachers of the targeted students have also been chosen to have authentic analysis for the case study.

III) Data Analysis:

A quantitative approach of data analysis (using SPSS software available in the school) has been employed to analyze the data statistically and truthfully. A qualitative approach has been used to analyze the interviews for both students and teachers.

IV) Findings
a. The Questionnaire

The results of the study have shown that (76) students have a positive tendency towards using their mother tongue in EFL classrooms (in general) and this percentage represents 48% of the total number of students in the study. The number of the students who have shown rejection of the use of Arabic in EFL classrooms was (53) students which represents 33% of the total number. The rest of the students (31) were neutral in their responses towards the questions in the questionnaire which might be a hider to come up with effective results of the study. Detailed analysis for each question in isolation might clarify the results (although some contradictions appeared in the analysis) of the study as follows:

1. 38% of the students prefer their teachers not to use Arabic during EFL classes, while 33% of them prefer their teachers to use the mother tongue in EFL classes.

2. 47.5% of the students feel more relaxed when they use Arabic while talking with their teachers, in comparison with 26% who object.

3. Unexpectedly, more than half of the students (55%) can understand the lessons better if teachers use their first language during the lesson. On the other hand, 26% reject this idea.

4. The percentage seems very close (39%=43%) about using Arabic when the lesson is somehow boring.

5. Another striking result show that 54% of the students feel that using Arabic helps them in expressing their opinions and feeling better than using English. Those who reject this idea only represent 26% of the total number.

6. 36% of the students prefer using Arabic when they ask their teachers questions in the classroom, while 39% prefer using English for the same purpose.

7. The use of Arabic or English during pair work activities shows a very close percentage (39% = 40%).

8. 41% of the students can understand the meaning of new words without the need to use a bilingual dictionary. In comparison, 38% believe they need to use a dictionary to understand new words.

9. Nearly 65% of the students agree that difficult exercises should be explained in Arabic, whereas 16% are sure this is unnecessary.

10. The percentages of students' attitudes toward using Arabic in explaining new grammar targets are very close. The results show 40 % with using Arabic for this purpose, while 41% reject the idea.

11. Surprisingly, 109 students (69%) find it a necessity to translate new English words into Arabic, whereas 23 students (14%) feel have an opposite opinion.

12. Of all students, 71 students (44%) say that the classroom instructions must be given in Arabic whereas 59 students (37%) refuse this way.

13. 68% of the students feel more relaxed when the instructions of the exams are translated into Arabic. On the other hand, only 29 students out of 160 say it shouldn't be done so.

14. The responses to this part of the questionnaire show some contradictions about the students' attitudes in comparison with the results in the first item. 54% of the students believe that using Arabic in EFL classrooms does not obstruct them from learning English in comparison with 33% who believe it is an obstacle for them.

15. 50% of the students say that the teacher must use Arabic in explaining and showing the differences between Arabic and English in comparison with 32% who say no.

b. The interviews

After analyzing the results of the questionnaire, the attitudes and responses needed to be clarified. So interviews with both teachers and students have been conducted to highlight some issues related to the research.

i. The interviews with teachers.

According to the teachers, the use of Arabic should be excluded from EFL classes at school as it is the only chance for them to use English. On teacher said: "*The only chance for students to use English is a 45-minute class a day! Why should I use Arabic?*" On the other hand, most teachers agree that sometimes they are forced to use Arabic, although rarely, for some reasons. One of the reasons for using Arabic is when they want to clarify abstract or ambiguous words. They believe that the level of the students should not affect their use of Arabic. On the contrary, most of them think "*it is a challenge to impose more English at classes and in the end it will help students to use English and only English.*" A teacher explained. Most of the interviews with the teachers show that they rarely allow students to use Arabic during classes as this will deprive them from the use of English and achieving fluency.

ii. The interviews with students

High achieving students reflect they do not feel motivated when their teachers use Arabic during classes. For them, the use of Arabic at classes is a hinder for accessing to that language. They say that their teachers use Arabic sometimes when they are stuck with low achieving students struggling to get the message through for new vocabulary, grammar target, or explain the instructions during classes. In comparison, low achieving students say that the use of Arabic helps them express themselves better and understand difficult words. They have explained that they are convinced that other students will laugh at them if they commit some mistakes. So their lack of confidence might be the major reason for using Arabic during classes.

V) Conclusions and recommendations

Arabic exists in EFL classrooms. Teachers are aware of the need to avoid too much use of Arabic in EFL classes admitting a systematic use of it in special cases. The attitudes of the students in the case study vary from one aspect to another, but many feel more relaxed and self confident when using Arabic in English classes. Their attitudes toward using Arabic seem to be habitual rather than systematic. So future studies must be carried out to explore this phenomenon thoroughly for beginners and should include both boys and girls. A lot of things can be done to avoid using the students' mother tongue in classes. I might be seen biased toward rejecting L1 in EFL classes, but two questions to those who advocate the use of it, could solve the problem. How can an Arab student learn other languages in many foreign countries in one year without having a zero-option use of their mother tongue there? Why don't our students learn English although they study it for twelve years or more?

REFERENCES

1. **Al-Nofaie, H.** (2010). " The attitudes of teachers and students towards using Arabic in EFL classrooms in Saudi public schools: a case study ", <u>Novitas-Royal (Research on youth and language)</u>, 4 (1): 64-95

2. **Alshammari, M.** (2011). The Use of the Mother Tongue in Saudi EFL Classrooms. <u>Journal of International Education Research – Fourth Quarter</u> 2011, 7/4: 95-102

3. **Atkinson, D.** (1993). *Teaching Monolingual Classes*. London: Longman.

4. **Atkinson, D.** (1987). The mother tongue in the classroom: a neglected resource? <u>ELT Journal</u> 41: 241-247.

5. **Auerbach, E.** (1993). "re-examining English only in the ESL classroom", in <u>TESOL Quarterly</u>, 27 (1): 9-32.

6. **Buckmaster, R.** (2000). First and second languages do battle for the classroom. The Guardian. Retrieved from: http://www.guardian.co.uk/education/2000/jun/22/tefl3

7. **Ford, K.** (2009), "Principles and Practices of L1/L2 use in the Japanese University EFL classroom", <u>JALT Journal</u>, 31/1: 32-80

8. **Hawks, P.** (2001). Making distinctions: A Discussion of the Use of the Mother Tongue in the Foreign Language Classroom, Hwa Kwang Journal of TEFL, Retrieved from: http://geocities.com/collegePark/Classroom/1930/Journal/May2001/page9.html

9. Krashen, S. (1982). *Principles and practice in second language acquisition.* Oxford, UK: Pergamon Press.

10. **Nation, P.** (2003). The Role of the First Language in Foreign Language Learning, <u>ASIAN EFI JOURNAL</u>, 5/2, article 1.

Appendix A

Students' questionnaire

تهدف هذه الاستبانة إلى معرفة موقف الطالب من جدوى استخدام اللغة العربية داخل الغرفة الصفية كوسيلة لتعلم اللغة الانجليزية والأسباب الكامنة وراء ذلك. أرجو الإجابة عن جميع الأسئلة بكل موضوعية وصدق؛ لأن ذلك يساعد على فهم احتياجات الطلاب والمشاكل التي تواجههم داخل الغرفة الصفية أثناء تعلم اللغة الانجليزية.

أولا: ضع إشارة(✓) في الخانة التي تتفق مع رأيك. يمكنك إضافة أي تعليق في المساحة المعطاة.

لا	نادراً	أحياناً	غالباً	دائماً		
					أفضل أن يستخدم المعلم اللغة العربية في حصص اللغة الانجليزية	1.
					أشعر بارتياح أكثر عندما أتحدث مع المعلم باللغة العربية	2.
					أستطيع فهم دروس اللغة الانجليزية أفضل عندما يستخدم المعلم اللغة العربية أثناء الشرح	3.
					أفضل أن يستخدم المعلم اللغة العربية إذا كان الدرس مملا	4.
					اللغة العربية تساعدني على التعبير عن آرائي ومشاعري بشكل أفضل من استخدام اللغة الانجليزية	5.
					أفضل أن أوجّه أسئلتي للمعلم باللغة العربية	6.
					أفضل أن أقوم بأداء التمارين مع زميلي في الصف باللغة العربية	7.
					أستطيع فهم معني الكلمات الجديدة فقط عندما استخدم قاموساً مترجماً	8.
					على المعلم أن يوضح التمارين الصعبة باللغة العربية	9.
					يجب شرح قواعد اللغة الانجليزية باللغة العربية	10.
					يجب ترجمة الكلمات الانجليزية الجديدة باللغة العربية	11.
					يجب إعطاء تعليمات الصف باللغة العربية	12.
					أشعر بالارتياح عندما تترجم تعليمات الامتحان باللغة العربية	13.
					استخدام اللغة العربية يعيقني من تعلم اللغة الانجليزية	14.
					على المعلم أن يستخدم اللغة العربية لتوضيح أوجه التشابه والاختلاف بين اللغة	15.

					العربية والانجليزية	

ثانياً: اذكر الأسباب التي تدفعك الى استخدام اللغة العربية أثناء حصص اللغة الانجليزية

....

....

....

....

....

....

....

....

....

....

....

....

....

ثالثاً: اذكر الأسباب التي تدفعك إلى تجنب استخدام اللغة العربية أثناء حصص اللغة الانجليزية.

....

....

....

....

....

....

....

....

....

....

....

....

....

شكراً على تعاونك

Appendix B

Interviews

A. Teachers' interview

1. The use of the mother tongue should be excluded from EFL classes. Do you agree? Why?

2. Do you use Arabic in your classes? If so, for what purposes?

3. Do you think that your students' level affect the amount of Arabic you use during classes?

4. Do you think that using Arabic is a sign for less creative teaching?

5. Do you allow your students to use Arabic in EFL classes? Why? Why not?

B. Students' interview

1. Do you feel motivated when your teacher uses Arabic in EFL classes?

2. Does your teacher use Arabic in EFL classes?

3. Do you think Arabic helps you to learn English?

4. When do you prefer your teacher to use Arabic?

5. When do you use Arabic in EFL classes?

1. هل تشعر بالحماس عندما يستخدم المعلم اللغة العربية داخل الصف في حصص اللغة الانجليزية؟

2. هل يستخدم معلمك اللغة العربية في حصص اللغة الانجليزية؟ متى؟

3. هل تعتقد أن استخدام اللغة العربية يساعدك على تعلم اللغة الانجليزية؟

4. متى تفضل أن يستخدم المعلم اللغة العربية في حصص اللغة الانجليزية؟

5. متى تستخدم اللغة العربية في حصص اللغة الانجليزية؟